DOVER CAST

JONATHAN COAD

INTRODUCTION

DOVER CASTLE, *one of the mightiest fortresses in western Europe, guards the English end of the shortest sea crossing to the Continent. Its location, overlooking the Straits of Dover, has given it immense strategic importance and has ensured that it has played a prominent part in national history. Its shape was largely determined by a pre-existing Iron Age hillfort, while within its walls stand a Roman lighthouse and an Anglo-Saxon church, the latter probably once forming part of an Anglo-Saxon* burgh *or fortified town.*

There has been a castle here since November 1066. That month, Duke William of Normandy's forces, fresh from victory at the Battle of Hastings, constructed the first earthwork castle before continuing their march on London. The castle was to retain a garrison until October 1958 – an 892-year span equalled only by the Tower of London and Windsor Castle.

During its medieval heyday this was very much a frontier fortress, looking across to the frequently hostile lands of the counts of Flanders and the kings of France. Under Henry II the castle was rebuilt, incorporating concentric defences and regularly spaced wall towers, a combination then without parallel in western Europe. In 1216 it successfully withstood a prolonged siege. By the 1250s its medieval defences had assumed the extent and shape which they retain to this day and the castle, on its cliff-top site, formed a highly visible symbol of English royal power.

After declining in importance from the sixteenth century, the castle was modernised and its defences extended in the 1750s and again during the Napoleonic Wars. Further alterations and additional gun batteries added in the 1870s enabled the castle to retain the role of First-Class Fortress almost until the end of the nineteenth century.

During both world wars the castle was rearmed, but perhaps its finest hour came in May 1940. In that month Vice-Admiral Bertram Ramsay, in naval headquarters deep in the cliff, organised and directed the successful evacuation of the British army from Dunkirk. These same tunnels became in the 1960s a Regional Seat of Government in the event of nuclear war; only in 1984 were they finally abandoned.

BOTTOM LEFT *A medieval archer defending a castle with his long-bow. Scenes such as this occurred at Dover in 1216*
TOP RIGHT *A member of the Dover garrison in the 1840s. Soldiers were based at Dover Castle from 1066 to 1958*
BOTTOM RIGHT *Prime Minister Winston Churchill and Vice-Admiral Bertram Ramsay pore over documents in the naval headquarters in the Dover cliffs during the Second World War*

ROMAN LIGHTHOUSE AND SAXON CHURCH

At the highest point in the castle stand two buildings which predate the castle – the remains of a Roman lighthouse and a Saxon church. The surrounding bank dates from the thirteenth century but underlies one dated by archaeologists to the mid-eleventh century, suggesting that this area could be the site of the first small castle built by William the Conqueror.

In the second half of the first century AD the Romans began to develop Dover as a port. To guide ships across the Channel they constructed three lighthouses. One, the Tour d'Odre, stood at Boulogne; the other two were at Dover, on high ground on either side of the small harbour. The foundations of the western lighthouse can be seen at Drop Redoubt on Western Heights on the far side of the town, while the eastern one still stands within the later castle, where it forms one of the most remarkable surviving structures of Roman Britain.

The Roman *pharos* or lighthouse was originally an octagonal tower with eight stepped stages, of which only four survive. It rose to a height of some 24m (80ft). Within its rectangular interior were a series of timber floors; at the top there was probably a platform for some form of brazier. After its abandonment by the Romans the tower became ruinous. Later its exterior was refaced, and between 1415 and 1437 the top was rebuilt as a bell-tower for the neighbouring church by Humphrey, Duke of Gloucester.

The Roman lighthouse as it may have appeared in the first century AD

Adjacent to the lighthouse stands the church of St Mary-in-Castro. Despite heavy restoration in the nineteenth century, it remains the finest late Saxon building in Kent, dating from around AD 1000. Its location, and the evidence of numerous Saxon burials found in a graveyard to its south, suggest that there was a pre-Conquest civilian settlement here. The church probably originally formed part of an Anglo-Saxon *burgh*, a fortified town within the Iron Age ramparts. The builders made extensive use of Roman tiles and the church retains its Saxon cruciform (cross-shaped) plan. Certain details in the interior, such as the vaults in the chancel and over the crossing, and the chancel windows, show that the church was modified in around 1200, probably by the same masons who had worked on the chapels in the keep.

By the early eighteenth century the church was in ruins. During the Napoleonic Wars (1803–15) it was used as a Fives Court and then as the garrison coal store. In 1862 it was restored by the architect Sir George Gilbert Scott and in 1888 William Butterfield completed the tower and added the unsympathetic mosaic decoration to the nave. The nearby church hall forms part of this mid-Victorian renaissance of this part of the castle; initially it was the schoolroom for the children of the garrison.

The surrounding medieval bank provides fine views. It was once topped by a medieval curtain wall linking to the eastern outer defences near Pencester's Tower and running westwards to Peverell's Tower via Colton's Gateway. The wall was demolished in 1772 but Colton's Gateway, built by King John, and the length of curtain wall beyond it, give an impression of the height of the missing sections. Beside the church hall are the earthworks of Four-Gun Battery, constructed in 1756.

The lighthouse and the church of St Mary-in-Castro from the west

Nineteenth-century engraving showing the church and lighthouse in ruins

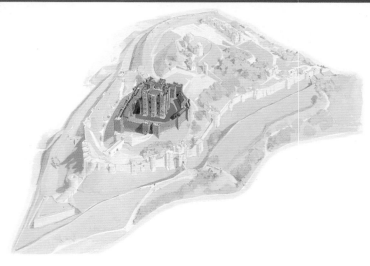

HENRY II's KEEP

In the 1170s and 1180s, Henry II's military engineer Maurice was to transform Dover. Central to the great rebuilding was the massive new keep, which ultimately was to be surrounded by a double ring of defensive walls, making Dover the first concentric medieval fortification in western Europe. The keep itself served multiple functions as a great storeroom, occasional residence of the monarch and his court, and ultimate stronghold during a siege. With few intervals and modifications, it was to retain a varied military role up to 1945.

The first line of defence beyond the keep were the curtain walls and towers of the inner bailey, with its two strongly defended gateways. Within the courtyard a succession of buildings was later added for royal and garrison use. Today the inner bailey is lined with barracks constructed in the mid-eighteenth century, but many of these incorporate the remains of earlier medieval structures.

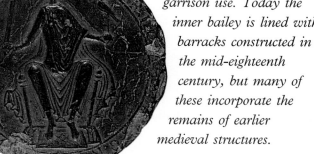

Henry II, the great castle-builder, here portrayed on his seal dispensing justice to his people

OPPOSITE *Henry II's great keep from the north-west. The strong defensive walls enclosed grand state apartments, two chapels and an ingenious well*

THE KEEP

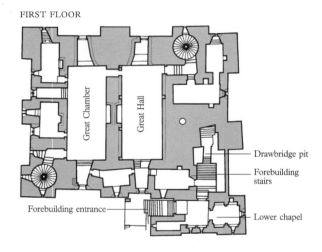

SECOND FLOOR

Principal bedchamber

Great Chamber

Great Hall

Garderobe shaft

Main entrance

Well

Drawbridge pit

Forebuilding stairs

Chapel of Thomas Becket

Sacristy

FIRST FLOOR

Great Chamber

Great Hall

Drawbridge pit

Forebuilding stairs

Forebuilding entrance

Lower chapel

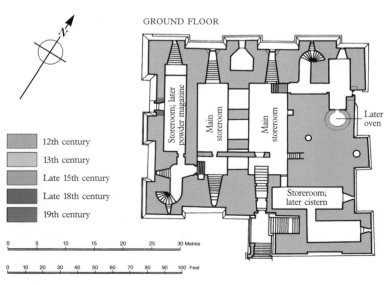

GROUND FLOOR

Storeroom; later powder magazine

Main storeroom

Main storeroom

Later oven

Storeroom; later cistern

12th century

13th century

Late 15th century

Late 18th century

19th century

| 0 | 5 | 10 | 15 | 20 | 25 | 30 Metres |

| 0 | 10 | 20 | 30 | 40 | 50 | 60 | 70 | 80 | 90 | 100 Feet |

Square or rectangular keeps forming the heart of a castle are characteristic of twelfth-century military architecture. Dover keep, as befitted a royal castle, was among the largest, roomiest and strongest in the country. It was also the last such royal keep to be built, and certain elements of its design point to a recognition that with the advent of powerful concentric defences there was less of a need to subordinate domestic convenience to defensive strength.

Dover keep stands some 25.3m (83ft) high; above its sloping plinth it measures 29.9m by 29.3m (98ft by 96ft), excluding the great forebuilding or protected entrance. Its walls vary in thickness from 5.2m to 6.4m (17ft to 21ft). Internally, there are three floors and the building is divided vertically by a cross-wall which rises the full height. Such a recitation of statistics conveys something of the sheer scale of this building, but only hints at its function.

The ground floor was always intended for storage, but the two floors above formed two separate sets of living accommodation. Linking these are two internal spiral staircases diagonally opposite each other, each set in the thickness of the walls. Approach to the building is up the heavily fortified stairs of the forebuilding which give direct access to the top floor. Here are the state apartments where the monarch stayed when resident in the castle. Lesser members of the royal household and less important guests would have been lodged on the first floor where there is similar but less grand accommodation.

In wartime the keep would have been defended by archers on the forebuilding towers and on the wall-walks behind the parapets. During peacetime, the keep mostly stood empty and bare of any furnishings. Medieval monarchs and nobles brought their own furniture and furnishings with them on their travels. Cart-loads of wall-hangings, tables, benches, household equipment and clothes would accompany them. These would be speedily installed and equally quickly removed when the visit ended.

When the keep was first completed in about 1190 the constable may have lived in it, but when Constable's Gateway was constructed in

This richly decorated interior suggests how the state apartments at Dover might have been furnished when the king was in residence. Edward IV, portrayed here, modernised the keep in the fifteenth century

the 1220s, constables would have lodged there instead (see page 23). A more convenient hall and chamber for the king were built in 1240 along the eastern side of the inner bailey, following which the accommodation in the keep would have diminished further.

Nevertheless, the keep was kept in repair and modernised from time to time, notably in the second half of the fifteenth century and again in 1539 when Henry VIII and Anne of Cleves stayed here. A last hasty modernisation before a royal visit took place early in 1625 when elaborate preparations were made to receive Charles I's bride, Henrietta Maria. Neither she nor her entourage were impressed with the castle, however. Thereafter, the keep served a variety of wartime uses: as prisoner-of-war accommodation early in the eighteenth century, then as barracks for troops. Late in the 1790s a new roof was installed on which heavy guns were mounted. The keep became an ammunition store and finally, during the Second World War, was used as military offices.

RIGHT *A medieval siege scene. The enemy advances with spears and scaling ladders, while the castle is defended by stone-throwers and cross-bowmen*

FOREBUILDING

The forebuilding forms the defensive entrance to the keep. Three towers straddle the steps; initially the spaces between them were unroofed, enabling defenders above to fire down on an approaching enemy, but these were roofed in the fifteenth century. The present steps are mostly modern. Above them can be seen the line of the original flight which did not turn through a right-angle before reaching the Keep Yard as now. At the lowest turn is a doorway leading directly into the basement. This apparently is an original feature. Although very well protected it would have been an unacceptable weakness in an earlier keep, one that was less well defended by outer walls and towers.

Within the first forebuilding tower is the lower of the two keep **chapels**, which still features its original rich decoration; the timber ceiling is modern. Adjacent is a small vaulted chamber with a window at its west end which presumably served as a porter's lodge or sacristy for the priest. The stairs continue up, passing a fifteenth-century doorway on the left then over the medieval drawbridge pit, before entering the middle tower and rising to the second-floor landing. At the head of the stairs is a guardroom and to the left is a fine doorway decorated with a moulded, round-headed arch and angle shafts with stiff foliated capitals. This is the ceremonial **main entrance** to the keep.

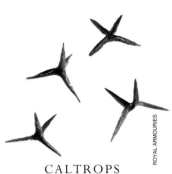

CALTROPS

These metal spikes were thrown on the ground to maim enemy cavalry

The Great Chamber on the second floor of the keep as it might have appeared soon after completion in the twelfth century

A rose, emblem of Edward IV, carved in one of the keep fireplaces

THE STATE APARTMENTS

The entrance passage shows clearly the great thickness of the outer wall of the keep; within its thickness to the left is the well chamber. The doorway and window were modernised in the fifteenth century but the **well** is an original and vital feature, deliberately made accessible at second-floor level only in case the basement was mined and captured during a siege, as indeed was to happen at nearby Rochester in 1215. The well had to be cut some 122m (400ft) deep to reach water. This in itself was a prodigious engineering feat, but Dover keep is also notable for having originally had a piped water supply to the lower floors from the well chamber – the remains of the two lead pipes can still be seen to the left of the well-head.

The two main second-floor chambers are still much as completed around 1180. However, their windows were enlarged in the fifteenth

century when new fireplaces were also added, some of the latter decorated with Edward IV's badge of the rose *en soleil* (an open rose). The original fireplaces were probably in the outer walls. At this stage, too, the door linking the two main chambers was repositioned. Both rooms are notable for their lofty vaulted ceilings. These were inserted in 1799 to allow guns on the roof, but they almost obscure the medieval mural (wall) gallery which runs round the upper levels and which once gave additional ventilation. The heavy timber floors probably date from the eighteenth century.

The first of the main rooms you enter from the forebuilding is the medieval **Great Hall**, the gathering place for those awaiting audience with the king. From here, they would be summoned to the presence of the monarch in the **Great Chamber** beyond. Here the king would hold court, confer with his chief officials, issue instructions, hear petitions and dispense justice.

In their heyday the rooms would have been richly decorated with wall-hangings, and would have provided the setting for entertainments and banquets.

The necessity of condensing what was in effect a small medieval royal palace within strong defensive outer walls led to some complicated planning. The great thickness of the outer walls allowed space within them for **garderobes** (latrines) for each of the principal rooms. Most people would have lived, eaten and slept in the Great Hall; only the monarch would normally have had a measure of privacy. Off the Great Chamber are two small rooms; both have fireplaces, modernised in the fifteenth century, and one has its own garderobe. It is tempting to suggest that this latter set of rooms could have been the sleeping quarters of the monarch on his visits. An exhibition in the Great Hall and Great Chamber recreates the preparation required for the arrival of Henry VIII and his court in March 1539, showing how the then empty medieval castle would have been temporarily transformed into sumptuous royal apartments.

The southern ends of the Great Hall and Great Chamber are connected by a corridor within the wall which may have done duty as a servery. Probably its more important use, however, was to link the king's apartments with the second-floor chapel in the upper part of the forebuilding.

A reconstruction illustration of the reception of Henrietta Maria in the Great Chamber at Dover in 1625, shortly before her marriage to Charles I

TERRY BALL

CHAPEL OF THOMAS BECKET

Before you reach the chapel there is a tiny **sacristy** for the priest, still with its original stone benches. The chapel itself has a small nave and chancel and is twice the size of the one below. Both sacristy and chapel are notable for the richness of their carving: the vault ribs with dog-tooth ornament, the arcaded walls, the shafts and columns with foliated capitals and the chancel arch enriched with chevron decoration. A later doorway in the north wall of the chapel dates from the fifteenth-century modernisation, but nowhere else in the keep is it possible to see so much unaltered work and to come so near to understanding the faith of the original builders. Later the chapel was dedicated to Thomas Becket, the archbishop murdered in Canterbury Cathedral by four of Henry II's knights a few years before the king began his great reconstruction of Dover.

THE ROOF

A doorway beside the main entrance to the Great Hall leads to one of the spiral staircases. Climb this to the roof. On the way, a narrow opening leads to a wall passage. This once overlooked the Great Hall and provided additional ventilation and light. However, the insertion of the vaults in 1799 obscured its original purpose.

The keep lies at the heart of concentric rings of defences

LONG-BOW

The main weapon of
English medieval archers,
who were famous for their
accuracy and rate of fire.
The arrows had an
extreme range of over
400m (1300ft)

CROSS-BOW

This fired an arrow with
great velocity, but the time
taken to tension the bow by
means of the windlass
meant the rate of fire
was slow

From the top of the keep are magnificent views in all directions and this is the best place to appreciate the huge scale of the castle. From here too can be seen some of the other fortifications which ringed Dover in the nineteenth century. On the hill west of Dover town are the immense earthworks of the Western Heights defences, and beyond the twentieth-century barracks north of the castle can be seen parts of Fort Burgoyne, begun in 1860.

The existing flat roof of the keep dates from 1799 when its construction allowed the mounting of heavy guns here; the existing surface is modern. Traces of these gun emplacements remain on the east side. Most of the crenellations are a restoration dating from the early 1930s. The eighteenth-century chimneystacks were demolished in 1898 when a huge cast-iron water tank was built here.

FIRST FLOOR

Return down either of the spiral stairs from the roof to the first floor. Here the layout is a near mirror-image of the state apartments above. There is the same sequence of **Great Hall** and **Great Chamber**, with extra rooms contrived in the thickness of the outer walls. Decorative detail here is notably less elaborate and, unlike the arrangements in the state apartments, the chapel on this floor can only be reached through the forebuilding. This level lacks the grand approach of the floor above and was clearly intended for less important officials and visitors.

The heavy timber framing in the Great Hall dates from the thirteenth century, when it was added presumably to strengthen the floor above. It in turn was largely encased in brick during modernisation works in the fifteenth century.

On this floor a doorway off the north-east spiral stair leads to two fine vaulted rooms placed immediately below the upper landing and forebuilding guardroom. Although the thickness of the vaults would have deadened the sounds of activity above, the occupant may have felt, rather than heard, the thud of the drawbridge being raised and lowered nearby.

THE BASEMENT

This is at ground level and was presumably always intended for storage. For most of its life it was probably little used. But when the castle was garrisoned for a siege – as in 1216 (recreated in the current exhibition) – it would have contained both provisions and munitions: sacks of corn, dried foodstuffs, barrels of ale, firewood, arrows, long-bows and cross-bows, as well as (perhaps dismantled) stone-throwing engines and their missiles. Without such resources – the modern equivalents of which were last stockpiled in the castle as recently as 1940 – no garrison could hope to withstand a siege.

The immense solidity of the keep is readily apparent at this level where the two main rooms, linked by three arches in the cross-wall, are smaller on account of the greater thickness of the outer walls.

On the south side is one of the few original windows to escape modernisation in the fifteenth century. Probably contemporary with the later windows are the remains of the cross-wall at the southern end. This would have sub-divided the storage space, probably for better security. The well-protected southern entrance with its series of barred doors was used as the main entrance for stores. In the fifteenth century a further door was added in the north-east angle of the keep, and just inside the lobby an **oven** was constructed. This was almost certainly for bread-making and is the only evidence we have for any cooking being carried out within the keep. It seems most likely that there was always a separate, detached kitchen in the south-east corner of the inner bailey.

*Dover Castle from the
Norfolk Towers, showing
the medieval barbican
protecting King's Gateway.
Behind, dominating the
centre, is Henry II's keep*

DOVER MUSEUM

ABOVE *A sentry stands
guard in the gateway of the
barbican; a watercolour of
about 1840*

BELOW *Reconstruction of a
scene inside one of the mid-
eighteenth-century Keep
Yard barracks. Georgian
soldiers slept two to a bed*

THE INNER BAILEY

The inner bailey walls protected the area known as Keep Yard. This was always the busy hub of castle life, and from very early on buildings lined the curtain walls. Keep Yard saw the comings and goings of monarchs and courtiers, ambassadors and royal messengers, soldiers and prisoners, tradesmen and merchants. Pack-horses, supply carts and baggage trains bringing furnishings for royal visits would have rumbled through the two gateways, as later did the wagons of the Board of Ordnance when the keep was used as a munition store.

The inner bailey, constructed at the same time as the keep in the 1180s, is notable for its sequence of fourteen square wall towers. These allowed defenders to send out flanking fire, adding greatly to the keep's defensive strength. Its two gateways – Palace Gate and King's Gate – are well protected between pairs of towers, the earliest use of such an arrangement in England. Both gateways originally had further outer defence works, or barbicans, but only the northern one survives. Its outer barbican gateway is carefully positioned so as not to align with the inner gateway, to blunt the rush of an attacking force.

The wall towers, which have been extensively refaced with new stonework, were reduced in height at the end of the eighteenth century to improve fields of fire. Later, in the 1850s, military engineers remodelled the wall-walks and parapets and modified the two gateways to incorporate lifting bridges.

Nearly all the existing buildings lining the inner bailey walls date from the early 1750s when they were constructed as barracks. These are among the earliest barracks to survive in the country. They are doubly notable as all of them incorporate medieval work from earlier buildings. The most important of these earlier buildings is Arthur's Hall, the great hall built for Henry III in 1240, providing the king with more modern and convenient accommodation than was available in the keep. The lower part of Arthur's Hall is still visible within the barracks on the eastern side of Keep Yard.

The most recent building, now the restaurant, was constructed in 1901 as a mobilisation store for the Royal Garrison Artillery reservists who would help man Dover's guns in wartime.

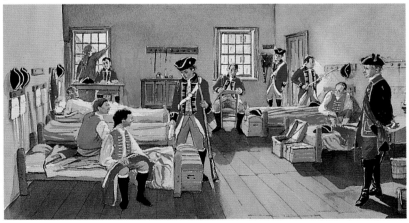

TERRY BALL

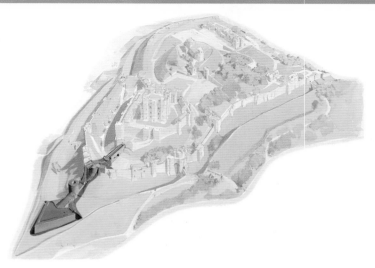

THE MEDIEVAL TUNNELS

The medieval underground tunnels at the northern tip of the castle form part of an extraordinary defensive system constructed by Hubert de Burgh after the siege of 1216. His was the first of several attempts to strengthen this area of the castle. Hubert's new defences were substantially modified in the eighteenth century, but the core of his underground work remains. The tunnels were designed to provide a protected line of communication for the soldiers manning the northern outworks, and to allow the garrison to gather unseen before launching a surprise sortie. Later, during the Napoleonic Wars, the tunnels were largely remodelled along with the outer defences, and were further modernised in the 1850s. In their date and complexity these tunnels are unique. Access to them is down a spiral stair beneath the bridge leading north from King's Gate barbican.

The Battle of Sandwich Bay in August 1217. Hubert de Burgh's ships decisively defeated French reinforcements under Eustace the Monk, ending all hopes of a French victory on land

OPPOSITE *A view down the medieval tunnels looking north towards St John's Tower*

An attack on a medieval castle, with miners demolishing the base of a tower

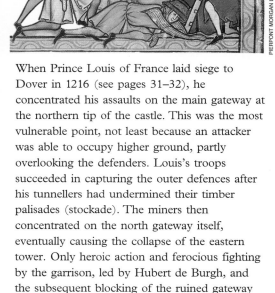

PIERPONT MORGAN LIBRARY/ART RESOURCE NY Ms 638 f 10v (detail)

Hubert de Burgh depicted in a Victorian painted window at Dover Town Hall

Hubert de Burgh was an able and efficient administrator and a courageous soldier who had a long and distinguished career serving Kings Richard I, John and Henry III. In 1204 he gained fame through his prolonged defence of Chinon Castle during John's retreat from Normandy, an experience that undoubtedly helped him during the great siege of Dover in 1216–17. In 1215 he was appointed Justiciar (chief minister) to the king, but in the 1230s powerful opposition, and loss of the king's support, led to his sudden downfall. He died in 1243.

RIGHT *The interior of the caponier leading to the spur. Carronades, which fired heavy shot a short distance, were ideal weapons for covering the moat*

When Prince Louis of France laid siege to Dover in 1216 (see pages 31–32), he concentrated his assaults on the main gateway at the northern tip of the castle. This was the most vulnerable point, not least because an attacker was able to occupy higher ground, partly overlooking the defenders. Louis's troops succeeded in capturing the outer defences after his tunnellers had undermined their timber palisades (stockade). The miners then concentrated on the north gateway itself, eventually causing the collapse of the eastern tower. Only heroic action and ferocious fighting by the garrison, led by Hubert de Burgh, and the subsequent blocking of the ruined gateway with tree trunks, saved the castle.

As soon as the siege ended, Hubert set about attempting to remedy the castle's structural weaknesses. A new and far more strongly protected gateway – Constable's Gateway – was built on the western side of the castle. To augment this, and to allow defenders to sally out on both sides of the castle, Fitzwilliam Gateway was constructed on the eastern side. At the northern end, the old gateway with its twin towers was blocked solid; these are now known as the Norfolk Towers. Beyond the moat Hubert built a substantial defensible earthwork or spur, from which defenders could pour fire on an enemy bent on attacking this part of the castle. The most ingenious part of the scheme was the underground link constructed between the castle and the detached spur.

Today, access to the tunnels and spur is gained down a spiral staircase constructed at the foot of the medieval bridge. The stairs date from the Napoleonic Wars, but at the bottom they join the steeply sloping tunnel dug in the chalk by Hubert de Burgh's miners during the major strengthening of the castle in the 1220s. Towards the bottom, the passage cuts through a rough-hewn cross-gallery which lies at a slightly higher level. This is probably one of the mining tunnels constructed by the besiegers in 1216. A little further on, an iron grating in the floor reveals a vertical shaft leading down to a still deeper tunnel of early nineteenth-century date. This provided a lower tier of communication to the outer defences.

Originally, the medieval tunnel emerged at this point through the castle bank into a short roofed passage terminating in St John's Tower. This three-storey tower was constructed by Hubert de Burgh in the middle of the moat. From its parapets, which were to be remodelled in the 1750s, bowmen could command the spur, while from its two sallyports defenders could pour into the moat. On the north side of the tower a drawbridge, protected by a portcullis, connected with a short bridge leading to a tunnel into the spur. Within the spur itself, the medieval tunnel divided into three passages, all except one of which are now blocked. These gave the defenders protected access to all parts of this northern defence work.

It is possible to see traces of all the medieval access arrangements here, but, with the exception of St John's Tower, the passage across the moat is in fact an adaptation of the defences carried out by Georgian military engineers during the Napoleonic Wars. Their

achievement was even more remarkable than that of their medieval predecessors. North of St John's Tower the medieval arrangements were largely replaced by a two-storey brick-vaulted caponier (a protected communication way), largely completed by 1804. Along this, firing loops on both sides allowed the defenders to sweep the moat with carronades (large-bore, short-range naval guns) and muskets. At the far end of the upper floor is a falling door which could cut off access below into the spur itself. Today the lower passage is reached by descending the modern timber stair in St John's Tower. At the end of the caponier a spiral stair, overlooked by firing loops from the upper floor, ascends to the level of the medieval tunnel.

The one surviving medieval branch passage leads down to a Napoleonic guardroom protecting a doorway leading out to the rear of the spur. This guardroom is notable for its firing loops and for the ingenious series of lever-controlled doors which allowed the guards to control entry. If necessary they could divert a hostile body of men into a walled enclosure where they could be shot from above.

Aerial view of the Norfolk Towers and part of the spur with the redan, showing the elaborate nature of these northern defences

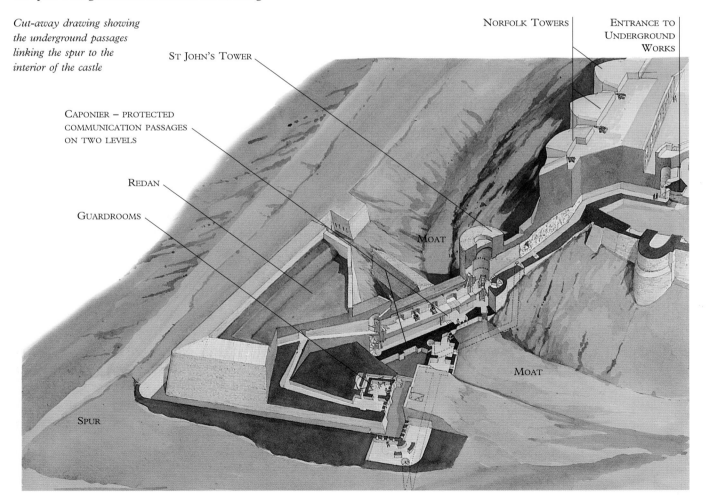

Cut-away drawing showing the underground passages linking the spur to the interior of the castle

NORFOLK TOWERS

ENTRANCE TO UNDERGROUND WORKS

ST JOHN'S TOWER

CAPONIER – PROTECTED COMMUNICATION PASSAGES ON TWO LEVELS

REDAN

GUARDROOMS

MOAT

MOAT

SPUR

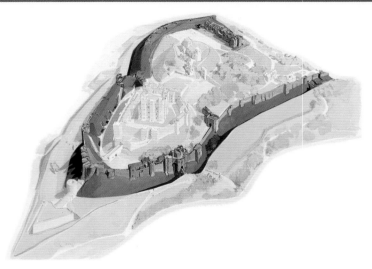

THE BATTLEMENTS WALK

Henry II's rebuilding campaign, begun in the 1180s and completed by his successors Kings John and Henry III, made Dover Castle one of the most powerful of all medieval castles. This great strength was due to the successive layers or rings of defensive walls protecting the keep in the centre. This is the earliest use of such concentric defences on a castle in western Europe. These fortifications were to be augmented by artillery outworks in the eighteenth and nineteenth centuries, most notably during the 1790s when attack by France was widely expected. The Battlements Walk follows the outer line of the medieval fortifications and gives stunning views over the castle's defences and surrounding areas.

For ease of use, the Walk is divided into an eastern route, starting by the entrance to the Medieval Tunnels, and a western route, starting by Canon's Gateway. It is possible to complete the whole circuit, on the way taking in Admiralty Look-out and the Secret Wartime Tunnels.

King George III (1760–1820). Wars during his reign led to an extensive modernisation of Dover's defences

OPPOSITE *The western defences of the castle. To the left is Constable's Gateway, in the centre Peverell's Gateway. The inner and outer medieval walls are clearly visible; dominating all these is Henry II's great keep*

EASTERN BATTLEMENTS WALK

The features highlighted in bold in this section can all be found on the plan of the castle (see inside back cover).

The Walk begins immediately to the east of the entrance to the Medieval Tunnels where a gun ramp leads up to the rampart. Gun ramps are prominent features of these artillery defences, as guns and their timber carriages were normally stored under cover in peacetime and would only be brought out on to the ramparts during hostilities. The wide earth ramparts from here to Avranches Tower were constructed in the 1750s by the military engineer John Peter Desmaretz, who was also responsible for the barracks lining the inner bailey. The ramparts were designed to mount heavy guns and help the medieval walls withstand the shock of artillery bombardment. Here, as elsewhere, the medieval wall towers were cut down to give the guns a clear field of fire, but the actual curtain wall remains substantially as built by Henry II and King John.

Turning left at the top of the gun ramp, you can see the whole of the northern tip of the castle as well as appreciating the layered system of defences, whereby each line of defence is overlooked by a higher one behind it. The old northern entrance, blocked in the 1220s and now known as the **Norfolk Towers**, is backed by brick casemates dating from about 1800. These provided accommodation for soldiers and a platform for guns aimed through embrasures overlooking **St John's Tower** and the **spur**. The arrow-shaped brick emplacement or '**redan**', which stands on the spur, was built in the 1790s to raise a further layer of guns to counter attack from the north. Beyond it stretches the spur itself, its shape defined by the brick parapets which provided a measure of protection for the defending troops. The low concrete wall or parapet on the western side was added in 1940 after the Dunkirk evacuation, as part of the defences against a possible invasion. It was designed to protect troops controlling the Deal road. The triple line of concrete anti-tank defences on the western shoulder of the spur are part of these same defence works.

Returning down the gun ramp, the road leads past **Fitzwilliam Gateway**, constructed in the 1220s. Its beak-shaped towers mirror the Norfolk Towers and are best seen from outside

ROYAL ARMOURIES

CANNON BALLS

Early cannon balls were made of stone, but these were superseded by cast iron in the sixteenth century. Cannon balls only became obsolete in the 1850s, with the introduction of explosive shells

Dover Castle from the east. The concentric medieval defences are well defined in this view, as are the later artillery earthworks

ABOVE *Bell Battery,
constructed in 1756*

ABOVE LEFT *Gun drill
training in the 1850s. This
photograph was probably
taken at Woolwich Arsenal,
but similar scenes would
have occurred at Dover*

the castle. The gateway lacks the formal grandeur of Constable's Gateway and has always very much been the 'back door' to the castle, a place of discreet entries and exits, where troops could gather and sally out unexpectedly in times of siege. Perhaps surprisingly, the late thirteenth-century Statutes or Rules of Dover Castle stipulate that this was the gate to be used by the king if he arrived unexpectedly after dark. Like Constable's Gateway, the rear of the main inner entrance once had living accommodation above it, but only fragmentary remains of the main chamber still survive. Originally a covered bridge crossed the outer moat to the gateway in the outer bank. During the Napoleonic Wars military engineers largely rebuilt the bridge to incorporate a caponier (communication passage) beneath it, from which troops could fire along the moat in both directions. The present steps, gates and brick parapet date from army alterations in the 1930s.

South from Fitzwilliam Gateway, the road along the inner moat passes below the formidable walls of the inner bailey, its square towers characteristic of Henry II's work of the 1180s, before being confronted by the menacing embrasures of **Bell Battery**, constructed in 1756. The road itself dives below Bell Battery in a tunnel, but before then a path to the left leads to steps to **Avranches Tower**. The castle plan shows that at this point the northern section of the eastern moat overlaps the southern stretch, from which it is possible to suggest that the Iron Age hillfort may once have had an entrance

here. This potential weakness was remedied by Henry II's engineers, who constructed powerful defences at this point: the polygonal Avranches Tower and the adjacent stretch of curtain wall between them have over fifty arrow loops in two tiers.

Georgian and Victorian military engineers further fortified this area. The narrow passage, once a sentry walk known as Avranches Lower Flank, joining Avranches to the site of Pencester Tower, is largely late eighteenth-century. From it, Georgian infantry could have poured a devastating fire over the outer defences, while in casemates below gunners would have raked the moat with grapeshot.

*Avranches Tower, a
powerful polygonal structure
built in the 1180s to control
an angle in the eastern
defences. Note the double
row of arrow loops*

From here there is a tremendous view south along the outer moat and over the outer defences. The medieval ditch was enlarged and lined with brick walls, and the outer curtain wall from here to the cliff edge was remodelled and backed by massive earth ramparts in the 1790s under the supervision of the Royal Engineer officer, William Twiss. Twiss was also responsible for the four great bastions lying beyond the outer moat – **Horseshoe, Hudson's, East Arrow** and **East Demi-Bastions**. All these were designed to bring extra guns to bear on the ground to the north-east of the castle and to provide flanking fire along the eastern line of defences. As with the northern outer defences, they were provided with communication tunnels under the main rampart.

The upper passage goes into a tunnel leading past the remains of the medieval **Pencester Tower** before emerging on to the ramparts by Bell Battery. From here the Battlements Walk leads along the top of the ramparts nearly to the cliff edge. The gun emplacements on this side support original smooth-bore guns mounted on replica carriages. At intervals between the gun emplacements are earth-covered 'expense' magazines. These were used in the nineteenth century for keeping supplies of gunpowder for immediate use, until stocks could be brought from the main powder magazines elsewhere in the castle.

Towards the southern end of the eastern rampart are three circular concrete bases. These were for anti-aircraft guns, installed during the Second World War and the last active weapons ever to be mounted at Dover Castle. West of these lies the vast **Officers' New Barracks**, constructed between 1856 and 1858 to a design by the architect Anthony Salvin. It originally housed forty-five bachelor officers of the Dover garrison as well as providing mess facilities. It now stands empty, a testimony to the size of the Victorian garrison here, and a reminder that by the end of the nineteenth century most of the open spaces within the castle were covered by barracks, storehouses and stables.

Beyond the fence, the hexagonal brick and concrete structure on the cliff edge was the base for a naval radar station, installed in 1943 to monitor shipping using the Straits. Information received here was relayed directly to the Admiralty headquarters in the cliff below. Nearby, steps lead down to the road, passing an underground powder magazine buried in the bank.

From here, a short walk down the road leads to Canon's Gateway and the start of the western sector of the Battlements Walk. On the way down, you pass on the left the Admiralty Lookout (see page 24) and the Secret Wartime Tunnels (see page 26). A little further down the road on the right is a rectangular stone-faced building with a single steel door. This is the top of the lift shaft installed in the 1960s to link with the Regional Seat of Government then being created in the tunnels below. Just outside it is a nineteenth-century triple spiral staircase giving access to the Georgian underground barracks.

The Officers' New Barracks – a photograph taken soon after their construction in the 1850s

DOVER MUSEUM

Canon's Gateway, constructed in the 1790s, is at the start of the western Battlements Walk

WESTERN BATTLEMENTS WALK

This section of the defences begins at **Canon's Gateway**, which was built in the mid-1790s to provide a more convenient and speedy link for troops between the castle and the harbour defences. Until then, all traffic on this side had to go through Constable's Gateway. Here, as on the eastern side, William Twiss remodelled the medieval outer wall, backing it with earth ramparts and incorporating casemates by Canon's Gateway. Just outside, in the moat south of the road bridge, stands the **Tudor Bulwark**, a small sixteenth-century gun platform. On the far side, partly shrouded by trees, can be seen the brick walls of **Shoulder of Mutton Battery**, constructed in the 1870s as part of a new system of cliff-top defences.

Inside the castle, the western battlements are best reached by passing the small group of military buildings which lie just to the north of Canon's Gateway. Hidden behind the grassy bank is one of the main **gunpowder magazines**. This dates from about 1800, but the earth bank was added about fifty years later to protect it from seaward bombardment. Behind it stands a group of barracks completed in 1913 for the **Royal Garrison Artillery** – the specialist troops responsible for the heavy guns of the fortress. On the opposite side of the road is the **Regimental Institute**, built in 1868 as a Canteen and Recreation Rooms; it was designed to tempt soldiers away from the taverns in the town below. The Institute was enlarged later in the nineteenth century and eventually included a library, reading rooms and billiard room; similar arrangements could be found at military stations throughout the British Empire. The small building to the north of it, with its ventilated roof, was constructed in 1895 as a bread and meat store.

The range of eighteenth- and nineteenth-century red-brick houses backing on to the western wall was used for a time as the **Cinque Ports Prison** (see page 33). Here debtors condemned by the Lord Warden's court were jailed; inside are the remains of some of the cells. More recently the buildings were used as army married quarters. The site of the prison exercise yard is now partly occupied by the Royal Garrison Artillery barracks.

Oil painting of the castle from the west by Arthur Nelson, about 1767. At this date the small town of Dover was still clustered tightly round the harbour

DOVER MUSEUM

Peverell's Gateway, completed early in the thirteenth century

PRIVATE COLLECTION

DOVER PEOPLE
—4—
WILLIAM TWISS

Portrait of Twiss by Sir Thomas Lawrence

Much of Dover Castle's present appearance is due to the work of William Twiss during the Napoleonic Wars. He created most of the massive outer defences, strengthened the top of the keep and built the underground barracks (the 'Secret Wartime Tunnels'). From 1792 he served as Commanding Engineer for the Southern District and in 1809 was promoted to Colonel Commandant of the Royal Engineers. Elsewhere in Dover he was responsible for the fortifications on Western Heights, including the Grand Shaft with its remarkable triple staircase.

Drop Redoubt overlooking the town of Dover. This fort is the easternmost part of the Western Heights defences. Begun in 1804, it was modified in the 1860s

Uphill from the Cinque Ports Prison the medieval wall and its towers come fully into view. This part of the original defences, leading south from Peverell's Gateway to the cliff, was completed by King Henry III in the 1220s. Like the work of his predecessor King John, it is notable for the use made of D-shaped wall towers, in contrast to the rectangular ones favoured by Henry II's engineers. Such rounded towers were held to be less vulnerable to stone-throwing artillery and more easily covered by fire from defenders on the adjacent wall-walks. Many of the towers along this western side of the castle are named after former constables, their deputies or the medieval lords whose knights served castle-guard (a fixed period of service each year) at Dover.

The earth bank added here by William Twiss is far less massive than that on the eastern side of the castle. By 1800 new fortifications around the harbour and on Western Heights opposite meant that a serious attack with heavy artillery on the western side of the castle was unlikely. The bank here is therefore only a firing step for troops using hand weapons. **Hurst's, Say's** and **Gatton's Towers** all show signs of having been altered at the same time, probably to mount some of the small 12-pounder guns known to have been in the castle at this date. There is an excellent view over the wall of the extensive outworks and batteries that were constructed to protect the approach road to Canon's Gateway and to provide a second layer of defence on this side.

Ahead lies **Peverell's Gateway**, part of the defences built by King John early in the thirteenth century. From it, a now-vanished length of wall once ran to join the inner bailey near Palace Gateway. Originally it had a drawbridge on each side, so it could face either way in the event of part of the castle being captured. In the eighteenth century, after its military use was over, Peverell's Gateway was used for a time as part of the Cinque Ports Prison.

From Peverell's Gateway there are fine views of the formidable walls and towers of the inner bailey, dominating the outer defences at this point and in turn overlooked by the keep itself. Here too is a good vantage point to look across the valley to the hill beyond the town. Brooding over the houses are the stupendous earthworks of the Western Heights fortifications. Western Heights was first fortified with temporary defences at the time of the American War of Independence (1775–83), but these were to be swept away by the permanent fortifications that remain today, largely constructed during the Napoleonic Wars. These were sited to control the Folkestone road and to prevent an enemy encircling the town and harbour from the west. They were the largest fortifications to be built in Britain during the Napoleonic Wars. Along with other contemporary works in the castle, they stand testimony to the importance attached by the government to securing Dover from invasion. The citadel of Western Heights is now a prison.

Looming beyond Peverell's Gateway is **Constable's Gateway**, inserted into the curtain wall by Hubert de Burgh between 1221 and 1227 to replace the old north entrance. The core of Constable's Gateway is one of King John's towers which was cut down and remodelled to form the entrance passage, protected at the front by a drawbridge. Two additional D-shaped towers set back-to-back, and two further towers on either side, made it possible to bring a powerful flanking fire to bear on an enemy approaching the entrance. This is one of the most elaborate castle gateways in the country, born of the shock of siege and near defeat.

Linking the towers to the rear of the gateway were a hall, chamber and further quarters for the constable, who was lodged here personally with his household to ensure the safety of the castle. Evidence of this medieval accommodation can be seen over the rear archway, although the flanking buildings are extensions of 1883, added to provide more spacious accommodation for a Victorian general.

Across the drawbridge is a barbican or defended outwork. This is medieval in origin but was extensively remodelled during the Napoleonic Wars when a powerful brick caponier (communication passage) was built beneath the bridge to allow cross-fire along the moat. To guard against a French bombardment of the gateway from the north-west, Twiss also constructed the great blunt-ended **Constable's Bastion**, thrusting out from the hillside to the south-west and capable of mounting four heavy guns.

From Constable's Gateway it is a short distance to the Norfolk Towers at the northern tip of the Battlements Walk. The route takes you past the 1883 stables and the final two towers of the outer curtain. These are **Crevecoeur** and **Godsfoe Towers**, again the work of King John. The area immediately to their rear may be the site of the King's 'new hall', referred to in a document of 1214.

A 1787 view of Constable's Gateway from the north showing the poor condition of this part of the outer walls

1205–14	
1221–27	

0 metres 10 20
0 feet 30 60

bridge

LEFT *Constable's Gateway, constructed in the 1220s to replace the old north gateway damaged in the great siege*

ABOVE *Plan showing the complex arrangement of towers that made up the strongly defended gateway*

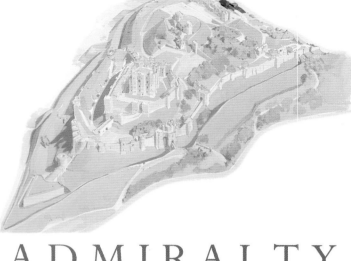

ADMIRALTY LOOK-OUT

Throughout most of Dover Castle's military life, the high cliff forming its southern boundary was sufficiently impregnable not to need any additional defences. On occasions from the sixteenth century onwards, temporary gun batteries were positioned near the edge to allow plunging fire on hostile vessels approaching the harbour from the east. However, with the development of more powerful weapons in the mid-nineteenth century and the need to protect an expanding harbour, permanent gun batteries were placed along the cliff edge for the first time in the 1870s. Between 1871 and 1874 East Demi-Bastion was re-equipped with two of the new rifled muzzle-loading guns, while Hospital Battery, Shot Yard Battery and Shoulder of Mutton Battery were constructed to mount a further thirteen heavy guns. Advances in centralised fire-control for such guns led to the conversion in 1905 of the by then obsolete Hospital Battery into a Fire Command Post for the harbour guns. In 1914 this was joined by the Admiralty Port War Signal Station, which controlled shipping movements into Dover Harbour. These two installations played notable parts in both the First and Second World Wars.

Vice-Admiral Ramsay on the cliff balcony

Admiralty Look-out stands on the cliff edge and is distinguished by its tall naval flagstaff used for signalling to shipping. The flat reinforced concrete roof and the blast-walls to the rear were added in 1941 as a protection against air attacks. A modern external stair leads to the roof, from which there are spectacular views over the cliffs and harbour and, on clear days, across to the coast of France.

The structures beneath the protective roof await conservation and are not yet open to visitors. The yellow brick buildings are the Fire Command Post of 1905 and the Port War Signal Station of 1914. These were added on top of part of the obsolete Hospital Battery of 1874. The present ground level means that much of the Hospital Battery to the west of these is buried by post-1945 infill.

To the rear of Admiralty Look-out is the site of the nineteenth-century garrison hospital after which the battery was named.

A little way down the road, a path on the left leads past the railings to the rear of Shot Yard Battery. When constructed in the early 1870s, this mounted two heavy guns. The emplacements can be seen through the trees. The magazine for ammunition is buried in the earthworks on the left. The flat-roofed brick building was built after the battery had become obsolete and was probably used for some form of wartime radio transmitting. To the right of the path is the circular top of one of the ventilation shafts constructed in the 1790s for the underground barracks. The path ends near Canon's Gate. At this point, visitors can either visit the Secret Wartime Tunnels or continue with the western Battlements Walk (see page 21).

IMPERIAL WAR MUSEUM

Royal Navy destroyers in Dover Harbour unloading troops from Dunkirk

BELOW *Admiralty Look-out and Port War Signal Station. The Look-out provides spectacular views over the cliffs and harbour*

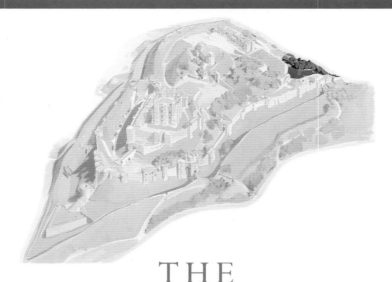

THE
SECRET WARTIME
TUNNELS

The Secret Wartime Tunnels are a complex web of underground rooms and passages which played a key role during the Second World War. They were later adapted to form the headquarters of one of a number of Regional Seats of Government, secure accommodation to be used in the event of a nuclear attack on Great Britain. However, the first tunnels here are considerably older and were built for a very different purpose.

At the end of the eighteenth century when Britain was at war with France, huge sums of money were spent fortifying Dover. The new defences required large numbers of troops who in turn needed to be housed. Conditions in the castle were extremely crowded with every available space in use, either for troop accommodation or for army stores, weapons and ammunition.

In 1797 a revolutionary solution was adopted. The Royal Engineers brought in a company of miners to start excavating a series of seven parallel tunnels running in from the cliff face some 15m (50ft) below the cliff top. These were linked at the rear by a communication passage and were provided with fireplaces, sanitation and a well. The first troops moved in during 1803. At their peak in the Napoleonic Wars, these totally secure underground barracks accommodated well over 2000 men. They are the only underground barracks ever built in Great Britain.

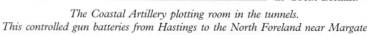

The Coastal Artillery plotting room in the tunnels.
This controlled gun batteries from Hastings to the North Foreland near Margate

OPPOSITE *The Anti-Aircraft Operations Room. The course of enemy aircraft was charted on the illuminated screens and co-ordinated on the plotting tables*

Military life in the underground barracks during the Napoleonic Wars

Two new grids of tunnels were excavated, one above and one below the existing complex. The upper set, known as Annexe, was intended primarily as a hospital. The lower set, known as Dumpy, largely replaced the headquarters function of the original eighteenth-century tunnels, known as Casemate. All the tunnels remained in full use until victory in 1945.

In the early 1960s most of the empty tunnels were again occupied and modernised, this time to prepare them to serve as a Regional Seat of Government following a nuclear attack. Elaborate air-filtering machinery, a huge new generator and oil-storage tanks, food stores, and communications equipment were installed, along with modernised kitchens and dormitories. The whole complex remained on the Secret List until abandoned in 1984.

The approach to the Secret Wartime Tunnels (a modern name recalling their most famous period of use) is down the sloping access ramp and tunnel cut in 1797. This leads to the terrace outside the main entrance to Casemate level. From here onwards, guided tours take visitors round the complex.

The seven large brick-lined tunnels – the original barracks – today reflect the extensive alterations which were carried out to adapt them for twentieth-century warfare. To give an impression of their appearance during the Second World War several of them have had contemporary equipment replaced. A high proportion of the tunnel space was devoted to the vital communication equipment needed to link the headquarters with the outside world. Deep within the cliffs was the main military

After the end of the Napoleonic Wars in 1815, the tunnels were little used. But just before the outbreak of the Second World War in 1939 they were turned into a bomb-proof headquarters for the fortress commander, the local coastal artillery and the Royal Navy's Dover Command. It was from these tunnels in late May 1940 that Vice-Admiral Bertram Ramsay inspired and directed *Operation Dynamo*, the Dunkirk evacuation.

From June 1940 Dover Castle was once again a front-line fortress, facing across the Straits to German-occupied France. Garrison numbers rose as troops and defence works were poured into this part of Kent. As operations grew, additional tunnels became a necessity.

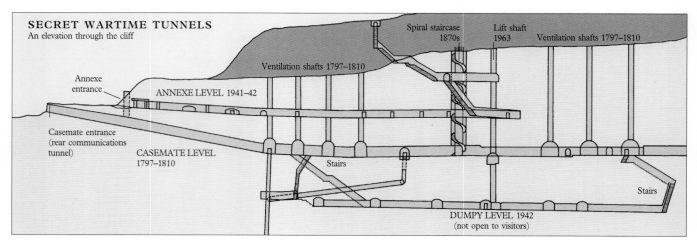

telephone exchange, installed here in 1941. The exchange served the entire underground headquarters, its manually operated switchboards manned around the clock, meshing Dover into the sinews of war, to the Admiralty, the War Office and the Air Ministry, to the fighter airfields, anti-aircraft batteries, naval bases, coastal artillery and radar sites.

Nearby is the General Post Office Repeater Station. Here massed ranks of equipment amplified telephone messages passing to and fro along the land lines. As with the telephone exchange, a small team of Post Office engineers was on duty day and night to ensure that there were no breakdowns.

The three main headquarters within the tunnels at the outbreak of the Second World War were the naval headquarters for the Dover Command, the Coastal Artillery operations room and the anti-aircraft operations room. This last has been partly reassembled, again making use of contemporary equipment.

By contrast, Admiral Ramsay's former naval headquarters today stands empty, enabling visitors to appreciate the huge scale of the Georgian underground barracks. In the walls are fireplaces which once provided some warmth for George III's troops quartered here, while lines on the walls and on the timber floor installed in the late 1930s show where naval office partitions were located. During the war years this tunnel was a warren of offices, with the Admiral's own quarters in the cliff front overlooking Dover Harbour and the Straits. (The cliff end was sealed by the Home Office in the 1960s.) Although it is silent now, little effort of imagination is needed to visualise this once-busy hub of naval activity, scene of so many momentous decisions.

The hospital tunnels, known as Annexe Level, lie above and slightly to the rear of the Casemate Level tunnels. The main entrance links directly to an ambulance lay-by on the road running up from Canon's Gateway. Inside, the differences in plan, scale and construction between the two sets of tunnels are at once apparent. The main tunnels of the 1790s are lofty, spacious chambers, lined with brick. Their 1941 equivalents are far more cramped and are lined with steel shuttering. In addition the hospital tunnels, unlike their Georgian predecessors, are laid out on a regular grid pattern.

The hospital comprised a carefully planned sequence of reception areas, wards, washrooms and latrines, galley and food store, and operating theatres. Most of the equipment on display is contemporary. The operating theatre, galley and mess are based on photographs showing them in use towards the end of the Second World War. Casualties mercifully were far lower than anticipated and, as a result, some of the tunnel wards were later given over to dormitories and mess accommodation for military personnel based at the castle.

During the 1960s, when the Regional Seat of Government was located in the lowest tier of cliff tunnels, the hospital level was re-equipped to provide accommodation. The bunk beds, wash room fittings and latrines largely date from this modernisation, but differ little from their wartime predecessors.

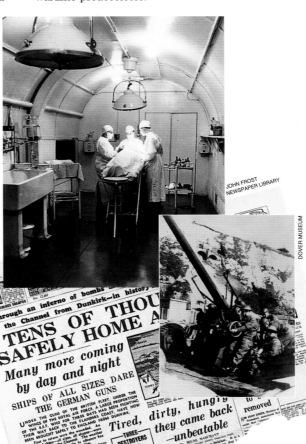

JOHN FROST NEWSPAPER LIBRARY

DOVER MUSEUM

DOVER PEOPLE
– 5 –
BERTRAM RAMSAY

Vice-Admiral Ramsay in his underground office

Bertram Home Ramsay (1883–1945) joined the Royal Navy in 1898. For much of the First World War he served in the Dover Patrol. In 1939 he was brought out of retirement and placed in command of naval operations in the Dover Straits. From his headquarters in the cliff tunnels he directed *Operation Dynamo* in May 1940. Four years later, as allied naval commander-in-chief for the Normandy invasion, Ramsay was responsible for the biggest and most successful invasion fleet in history. He was killed in an air crash in France.

TOP *Wartime photograph of the operating theatre in use.* LEFT *The* Daily Express *of 31 May 1940 reports the success of Operation Dynamo.* RIGHT *An anti-aircraft gun and its crew by Dover Harbour in about 1941*

THE HISTORY OF DOVER CASTLE

Turner's view of Dover (about 1825) deliberately exaggerates the height of the cliffs. The harbour at that time was restricted to the area to the extreme left of the painting

The extraordinary sequence of defences on this cliff top – the Iron Age hillfort, medieval royal castle, artillery fortress and Second World War headquarters – owe their existence to the need to protect and dominate the nearest landing place in England to mainland Europe. The valley of the River Dour is the only break in some 21km (13 miles) of high chalk cliffs. From the earliest times the river mouth provided shelter and a landing place, from which ultimately grew the present Dover Harbour.

THE FIRST NORMAN CASTLE

In November 1066, following his landing at  Pevensey just along the coast from Dover, Duke William of Normandy and his victorious army advanced on Dover. The inhabitants speedily surrendered and William spent eight days fortifying the site before marching on Canterbury. These early Norman defences have never been identified, but archaeological excavations suggest that they were probably centred on the Roman lighthouse and the Saxon church, and that they took the form of a bank topped by a timber palisade (or wall) surrounded by a ditch. Within a year they were to prove their worth when the garrison beat off an attack led by Count Eustace of Boulogne who had landed to aid the Kentish rebels.

HENRY II'S CASTLE

We know virtually nothing about Dover Castle between 1067 and the 1160s. Henry II became king in 1154 and was to prove himself one of the greatest of medieval castle builders. Royal accounts show Henry building or altering no less than 90 fortifications in England alone, with by far and away the largest expenditure at Dover.

In the 1160s and 1170s small sums of money were spent updating the existing defences. But between 1179 and 1188 expenditure rose to nearly £6000, creating much of the medieval castle which survives today. This work was largely carried out under the supervision of Maurice the 'Ingeniator', one of the most accomplished medieval military engineers in Europe. Maurice was responsible for the keep and the walls and towers of the inner bailey. He also began part of the outer bailey wall, and thus should be credited with being the designer of the first castle in western Europe to boast concentric defences.

THE GREAT SIEGE OF 1216

On Henry II's death in 1189 Dover Castle must have resembled a vast building site. Nevertheless, it was not until the loss of Normandy in 1204 that King John devoted substantial funds to completing the castle. Work was concentrated on the outer defences where the new building can be identified by the use of D-shaped wall towers. The defences were extended round from the north-east side down to Peverell's Tower. A now-vanished length of wall linked Peverell's Tower to the inner bailey near Palace Gateway, while the main outer gateway was built at the northern tip of the castle. By 1215 the fortifications were sufficiently advanced to make the castle defendable.

In the civil war between King John and his barons, Dover was to achieve legendary fame. In support of the rebels a French army under Prince Louis landed at Thanet in May 1216. In response John had barely sufficient time to provision Dover Castle and install 140 knights under Hubert de Burgh, Justiciar of England, before retreating to Winchester. By the autumn of 1216, only Windsor and Dover Castles in southern England remained in the king's hands.

At Dover, Prince Louis himself directed the siege, establishing his headquarters at Dover Priory in the town and his main camp just to the north of the castle on the higher ground. From here, great stone-throwing engines bombarded the outer walls while miners slowly tunnelled under the northern barbican. Nothing daunted, the garrison launched frequent sorties to attack their assailants, but the undermining of the barbican brought them to a halt and forced them to withdraw behind the north gate.

Again the French miners set to work, and this time brought down the eastern of the two gate towers. It seems that the garrison was well aware of the tunnelling, for the small tunnels which still exist within the castle are probably countermines, dug in the hope of intercepting the enemy miners. When the tower collapsed and the French poured into the castle, Hubert de Burgh and his knights were ready for them. In what was

William the Conqueror, who ordered the first medieval fortifications at Dover. (A seventeenth-century portrait)

The end of the siege of Dover Castle in 1216 is recorded in this Victorian painted window in Dover Town Hall

clearly bitter hand-to-hand fighting just within the ruined north gateway, the garrison fought back, ultimately forcing the French to retreat through the breach.

This was to prove the climax of the siege. For Louis, faced with an implacable and determined garrison, the siege was increasingly unsatisfactory. A truce was called early in the autumn but in October King John died at Newark Castle and his son, Henry III, was proclaimed king. At Dover the local truce held into the spring of 1217, but in May Louis returned to resume siege operations, aware that the castle had to be captured to secure his supply lines. Three days later, however, French forces were defeated at the Battle of Lincoln, effectively signalling the end of the war. Dover Castle, after a year of sieges and truces, remained uncaptured although badly damaged.

THE WORKS OF HENRY III

The siege of 1216–17 had exposed the vulnerability of the castle's northern defences. With Henry III's backing and initially under the personal supervision of Hubert de Burgh,

enormous efforts were made to overcome these weaknesses. The northern gateway, so nearly the castle's downfall, was blocked solid. In the moat beyond, engineers constructed St John's Tower which in turn overlooked a new spur or outwork to the north, designed to allow the garrison a better command of the high ground. The north gateway was replaced by the formidably powerful Constable's Gateway on the western side of the castle. Difficult anyway for an attacker to approach because of the sloping ground, the clustering of no less than six towers here made it one of the most powerful gateways in England. A secondary entrance, Fitzwilliam's Gateway, was built on the eastern side of the castle.

Apart from work on the three gateways, the outer curtain wall was completed from Peverell's Tower to the cliff edge, and a massive earth bank was constructed round the church and *pharos*. Initially this bank was topped by a timber palisade but this was replaced by a stone wall in the 1250s. Footings of the wall can still be seen. On the completion of these works Dover had reached the peak of its medieval power; its formidable series of concentric defences allied to its strategic location led the contemporary chronicler Matthew Paris to title it the 'key of England'.

ROYAL ARMOURIES

CROSS-BOW BOLTS

These were much shorter than long-bow arrows but were among the most feared of medieval missiles on account of their range and penetrative power

Dover Castle as it probably appeared in the second half of the thirteenth century following the completion of Henry III's works. As the first concentric castle in western Europe, Dover features a series of curtain walls and earthworks encircling the mighty keep

TERRY BALL

Within the castle, money was also spent on modernising the facilities. Documents mention repairing the oven in 1221, the addition of a new granary, and in 1234 the construction of a windmill to grind flour for the garrison. In 1240 a new hall and set of chambers for the king were completed on the south-eastern side of the inner ward. Later known as Arthur's Hall, the lower walls of this structure can still be seen today.

LIFE IN THE MEDIEVAL CASTLE

Dover Castle's primary role was that of a frontier fortress, its dominant position a symbol to passing shipping of English royal power. During peacetime it probably had a garrison of around a dozen knights, with further footsoldiers, warders and porters. Initially this garrison was raised by means of castle-guard, an unpopular and unreliable feudal duty whereby the larger baronial estates were bound to supply a knight for forty days' service each year. After the 1216 siege, castle-guard was replaced by money payments, allowing the establishment of a more permanent and professional garrison.

The castle was in the charge of a constable, first appointed during the reign of King Stephen (1135–54). A century later, to avoid disputes, the role of Lord Warden of the Cinque Ports was combined with that of constable. This dual role made the medieval constable's job a demanding one. As well as looking after the castle and providing hospitality for important officials, ambassadors and courtiers on their way to and from the Continent, he was responsible for the defence of the coastline of south-east England, for overseeing Channel shipping and for providing ships from the Cinque Ports when demanded by the king. The constable was also President of the Court of Shepway, the administrative heart of the Cinque Ports federation. In addition, most medieval kings stayed at the castle at some time during their reign; the constable was responsible for their comfort and safety.

To share the burdens of office a deputy constable was appointed, principally to look after the castle. In the early eighteenth century the constable, whose role by this time had become largely ceremonial, shifted his official residence to Walmer Castle. The deputy constable, however, still lives in Constable's Gateway.

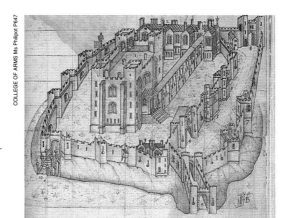

COLLEGE OF ARMS Ms Philipot P647

The keep and inner bailey by John Bereblock. This drawing of 1626 shows the towers of the inner bailey curtain wall before they were reduced in height in the eighteenth century. Note the pentice, or covered way, linking the keep to Arthur's Hall

THE CINQUE PORTS FEDERATION

BRITISH LIBRARY

The Barons of the Cinque Ports enjoyed numerous privileges including the right to carry the canopy over the new king at his coronation, as seen here at the coronation of Richard the Lionheart in 1189

From the second half of the thirteenth century the administration of the Confederation of the Cinque Ports was based at Dover Castle. This group of five port towns – Hastings, Romney, Hythe, Dover and Sandwich – had first banded together in the eleventh century to provide ships and men for the defence of the coast and the protection of cross-Channel trade. In return for this work – which was vital to the Crown before the establishment of a permanent Royal Navy – the towns were granted substantial privileges, including exemption from national taxation and external courts of justice. By the thirteenth century, however, the federation had become a powerful and occasionally lawless organisation. To introduce a measure of control, the government instituted the post of Warden to regulate the Confederation's affairs and to act as a link with the Crown. Henry III further strengthened royal control in the second half of the thirteenth century when he combined the post of Warden with that of the Constable of the Castle. From that time on, the appointment remained firmly in the hands of the monarch.

Since 1708 Lords Warden have used nearby Walmer Castle as their official residence, although they have continued to combine that role with the title of Constable of Dover Castle. Many distinguished public figures have held the title, including the Duke of Wellington (installed in 1829), Viscount Palmerston (1861) and Sir Winston Churchill (1941). Since 1978 the title has been held by H M Queen Elizabeth the Queen Mother.

DOVER EXPRESS NEWSPAPER

H M the Queen Mother at her installation as Lord Warden

THE CASTLE IN DECLINE

By 1500 the castle was becoming increasingly out of date as guns grew in size and power. While its strategic location and the convenience of its buildings ensured that it remained in use, the main defences were now sited at harbour level. In 1539 King Henry VIII and Anne of Cleves stayed in the keep, while Elizabeth I lodged in the castle in 1573. In 1624 elaborate preparations were made in the keep to receive Henrietta Maria of France on her way to marry Charles I. At the outbreak of the Civil War in 1642, Dover town sided with Parliament while the castle garrison supported the king. That August a small party of townsfolk daringly scaled the cliffs, surprised the garrison and captured the castle, which fell with hardly a shot fired.

At the Restoration of the monarchy in 1660, grandiose plans to quarter a substantial garrison in the castle were eventually reduced to the installation of seventeen gunners, probably based at Moat's Bulwark, the sixteenth-century gun battery at the foot of the cliffs. The castle itself remained largely uninhabited, the keep being used to house prisoners-of-war for a number of years at the end of the seventeenth century.

Moat's Bulwark in the eighteenth century

DOVER TRANSFORMED

This gentle decline was abruptly reversed in the 1740s. From then on, up until 1945, Dover castle was to have its defences modified and extended in every European war in which Britain was involved. The reason for this change in the castle's fortunes lay in Dover harbour below. In 1066 William the Conqueror had been able to land his foot soldiers and knights on a shingle beach at Pevensey. By the eighteenth century, heavy siege weapons were key components of armies and to bring these ashore required the use of a harbour. Dover harbour, the nearest to mainland Europe, made it a prime target for any power considering invading Britain. In 1744 the threat was a Jacobite invasion from Dunkirk; in 1805 it was Napoleon's Grand Army, and in 1940 Hitler's *Wehrmacht*.

From the sixteenth century onwards, Dover harbour had been protected by a series of artillery forts, such as Moat's Bulwark and Archcliffe Fort. These provided local protection against a direct assault by sea. By the 1740s, military planners feared that an enemy might land light forces in the area of Walmer or Hythe, who would then encircle Dover from the rear and capture the harbour by a landward attack. In such a context, Dover Castle had a vital new role protecting town and harbour from a landward assault.

In 1745 new barracks were built within the inner bailey to accommodate extra troops. In the 1750s the military engineer J P Desmaretz added further accommodation, part of which was situated in the keep. More importantly, in 1755 he strengthened the northern defences of the castle, remodelling the outer curtain from Avranches Tower to the Norfolk Towers to carry heavy artillery, modernising the medieval spur to accommodate infantry, and building two new gun batteries – Bell Battery and Four Gun Battery. All these works were intended to protect the castle from assault from the high ground to the north-east and were the first major additions to its defences for 500 years.

Modernisation was continued in spectacular fashion at the end of the eighteenth century,

Two queens who lodged at Dover Castle. ABOVE: *Anne of Cleves, fourth wife of Henry VIII.* BELOW: *Henrietta Maria, the French consort of Charles I, who was not impressed with her accommodation in the keep*

Queen Elizabeth's Pocket Pistol, a 12-pounder brass Basilisk (a type of cannon) cast at Utrecht, Holland in 1544 and presented by the Emperor Charles V to Henry VIII. It is known to have been at Dover as early as 1613

during the wars with Revolutionary and Napoleonic France, by Lieutenant Colonel William Twiss. Twiss completed the remodelling of the outer defences, adding the huge Horseshoe, Hudson's, East Arrow and East Demi-Bastions to provide extra gun positions on the eastern side, and constructing Constable's Bastion for additional protection on the west. Twiss further strengthened the Spur at the northern end of the castle, adding a redan or raised gun platform. By taking the roof off the keep and replacing it with massive brick vaults he was able to mount heavy artillery on the top.

To help troop movements between castle and town defences, Twiss constructed Canon's Gateway. He filled every available space within the castle with barracks and storerooms, and, when space ran out, he constructed the remarkable underground cliff barracks. In the midst of all this work, Twiss was also overseeing construction of the vast fortifications which still dominate Western Heights on the opposite side of the town. Designed to thwart an overland attack from the west, the addition of these new defences meant that Dover now had its two most vulnerable landward approaches well defended. All these works were at their height during the crucial years 1803–1805 when a French invasion was expected daily; at this time the town and castle were packed with troops.

The triumphal conclusion of the Napoleonic Wars saw a rapid reduction in Dover's defences; only a small garrison remained at the castle. But by the 1850s the introduction of steam-driven warships and troop transports, and the invention of vastly more powerful guns, led to an extensive programme of rearmament. Within the castle, King's Gate and Palace Gate were strengthened and the inner bailey wall-walk remodelled: the keep itself was reverting to its medieval use as place of last resort. These adjustments, however, offered only superficial improvements; in truth the new armaments had finally rendered Dover Castle obsolete as a major fortress. This was acknowledged in 1860 by the start of the construction of Fort Burgoyne on the high ground to the north-east of the castle. The new fort was intended to take over the functions of its medieval predecessor.

The castle itself continued in use as a garrison headquarters and the 1850s saw an extensive programme of barrack building, including Salvin's Officers' New Barracks which still dominate the southern part of the castle. Barracks continued to be built at intervals into the 1930s. In 1862 Sir George Gilbert Scott restored the ruinous St Mary-in-Castro for use as the garrison church.

The last major rearming was undertaken in the 1870s when a series of gun batteries was built along the cliff edge to protect the harbour below. Ammunition was stored in a large underground magazine constructed to the west of Salvin's New Barracks.

LEFT *Troops filing through Colton's Gateway – a watercolour painted in the 1840s*

Dover Castle from Western Heights. GB Campion's romanticised nineteenth-century watercolour largely omits the Napoleonic War fortifications. The soldiers in the foreground were probably stationed at Drop Redoubt or Grand Shaft Barracks

DOVER CASTLE IN THE TWENTIETH-CENTURY

The castle played a notable role in the two world wars of the twentieth century. The Fire Command Post on the cliff edge controlled all the guns around the harbour, while from the Port War Signal Station above, the Royal Navy directed shipping movements in and out of Dover harbour. In both wars the castle was armed with anti-aircraft guns and searchlights, supplemented during the Second World War with radar.

The castle's finest hour since the Great Siege of 1216 came in May 1940. By then the Georgian underground barracks had been converted into a command centre safe from air attack. From the easternmost casemate, Vice-Admiral Bertram Ramsay directed *Operation Dynamo*, the extraordinary evacuation of nearly 338,000 allied soldiers from the mole and beaches of Dunkirk. In saving the British army, the Royal Navy and merchant marine vastly improved Britain's chances of survival. Later that summer, as British supply convoys fought their way through the Straits of Dover and the Battle of Britain raged overhead, Dover Castle was provisioned to withstand a six-week siege in the event of a German invasion. Mercifully this never happened, but for the rest of the war the castle resumed its medieval role as a frontier fortress, and the battles fought in the air and sea earned this part of Kent the title 'Hellfire Corner'.

Dover Castle photographed by a long-range camera from German-occupied France during the Second World War

In 1941 a grid of tunnels known as Annexe was excavated above the existing Georgian network to form an underground hospital. Following an abortive attempt to extend a further grid to the rear of the Georgian tunnels, a third layer of galleries known as Dumpy was constructed below them in 1942. These formed a combined headquarters for the three services which remained operational until victory in 1945.

After the war, the army remained in the castle until 1958; five years later the whole of Dover Castle was handed over to the Ministry of Works for preservation. But the Cuban missile crisis of 1962, which brought the world to the brink of nuclear war, created yet another role for Dover Castle. For the next twenty-two years, the cliff tunnels were reactivated to form a Regional Seat of Government which would have controlled what remained of Kent and East Sussex after a nuclear attack.

Very few other medieval castles have had such a long and stirring history; none has undergone such a series of modernisations and adaptations to fit it for new forms of warfare. Dover Castle is interwoven into England's history, well meriting its medieval title, the 'key of England'.

SHELLS

Explosive shells such as these, fired from rifled muzzle-loading guns in the 1860s, replaced round shot fired from cannons

Winston Churchill (right of centre) watches an air battle from the Casemate balcony on 28 August 1940

FURTHER READING

Jonathan Coad, *Dover Castle*, London 1995

H M Colvin (ed), *The History of the King's Works*, vols 1 and 2, London 1963